Jimmy Carter

By United Library

https://campsite.bio/unitedlibrary

Table of Contents

Table of Contents 2

Disclaimer 4

Introduction 5

Jimmy Carter 8

Children and youth 10

Beginnings in politics 14

Presidency of the United States (1977-1981) 24

Foreign policy 38

Legacy 55

Diplomacy 60

Ideological positions 66

Personal and family life 71

Other books by United Library...75

Disclaimer

This biography book is a work of nonfiction based on the public life of a famous person. The author has used publicly available information to create this work. While the author has thoroughly researched the subject and attempted to depict it accurately, it is not meant to be an exhaustive study of the subject. The views expressed in this book are those of the author alone and do not necessarily reflect those of any organization associated with the subject. This book should not be taken as an endorsement, legal advice, or any other form of professional advice. This book was written for entertainment purposes only.

Introduction

Delve into the extraordinary life and legacy of James Earl Carter Jr. the 39th president of the United States in this comprehensive biography that traces his journey from small-town Georgia to the highest office in the land and beyond. James Carter's book offers a compelling portrait of a man who left an indelible mark on American politics and global diplomacy.

Born and raised in Plains, Georgia, Carter's early years were marked by a strong commitment to his family's peanut business and a growing dedication to civil rights and desegregation. After graduating from the U.S. Naval Academy and serving in the Navy's submarine division, he returned to Plains to revive the family business while actively supporting the civil rights movement in the racially charged South.

Carter's entry into politics saw him rise through the ranks, serving as a state senator and eventually as governor of Georgia. As a little-known candidate, he secured the Democratic nomination and narrowly defeated incumbent President Gerald Ford in the 1976 presidential election.

As president, Carter faced a number of challenges, including the energy crisis, stagflation and international crises such as the Iran hostage crisis and the Soviet invasion of Afghanistan. However, his administration achieved important milestones, such as the Camp David Accords, the Panama Canal Treaties, and the establishment of the U.S. Department of Energy and Department of Education.

Carter's post-presidential life was equally impactful, as he devoted himself to humanitarian causes, peace negotiations and human rights through the Carter Center. His Nobel Peace Prize in 2002 recognized his unwavering commitment to the promotion of peace and the eradication of infectious diseases.

This biography presents a vivid picture of a leader who continues to inspire generations with his dedication to public service, leaving a lasting legacy that extends far beyond his tenure. Whether you are a history enthusiast or seeking information about the life of a Nobel laureate and statesman, this book offers a captivating exploration of an extraordinary American leader.

Jimmy Carter

James Earl Carter Jr. (Plains, Georgia; October 1, 1924) is an American politician of the Democratic Party who was the thirty-ninth president of the United States (1977-1981); previously he had served as governor of the state of Georgia (1971-1975) and as a senator in the Georgia General Assembly (1962-1966). Carter was awarded the Nobel Peace Prize in 2002 for his efforts "to find peaceful solutions to international conflicts, to promote democracy and human rights, and to foster economic and social development".

His term as President of the United States was marked by important successes in foreign policy, such as the Panama Canal treaties, the Camp David peace accords (peace treaty between Egypt and Israel), the SALT II treaty with the Soviet Union and the establishment of diplomatic relations with the People's Republic of China, and experienced its most tense moments with the Iran hostage crisis. In domestic policy, his government created the Departments of Energy and Education and strengthened environmental protection legislation.

Since leaving the White House, he has dedicated himself to mediation in international conflicts and the support of humanitarian causes. In 1982, together with his wife,

Rosalynn, he founded The Carter Center, a non-governmental organization that fights for the advancement of human rights, mediation in international conflicts and has been present as an observer in different electoral processes.

Children and youth

James Earl Carter Jr. was born on October 1, 1924 in Plains, a small farming town near Americus, Georgia. Carter's ancestors came from southern England (his paternal family came to the American Colonies in 1635), and have lived in the State of Georgia for several generations. Carter has documented ancestors of his who fought in the American Revolution, and his grandfather, L.B. Walker Carter (1832-1874), fought in the Confederate States Army during the Civil War.

His father was James Earl Carter, a well-to-do agricultural entrepreneur who grew cotton and peanuts and exercised the traditional role of Southern landowner in the United States. Carter describes him as a brilliant farmer and a strict segregationist who treated black workers with respect and fairness. His mother was Bessie Lillian Gordy, a registered nurse at the Wise Clinic in Plains who passed on to her son her love of reading. Jimmy was the oldest of the couple's four children. In his childhood, during the Great Depression, the family moved to live on a farm his father had purchased, located in Archery near Plains. As Carter recounts in his memoir *An Hour Before Daylight: Memoirs of a Rural Boyhood*, on the farm, despite being one of the most prosperous families in the community, they lacked electricity and running water. Most of his neighbors were African American, sharecroppers or laborers on his father's farm, Carter was in constant contact with them, eating in their homes and, when his parents were away, spending the night at the home of Rachel and Jack Clark, employees of the family farm. This interracial contact was only possible on the farm, as the rigid legal code of racial segregation at school, church, and other public places was separate. On one occasion, Carter went to the movies in Americus with his best friend, A.D. Davis, and had to ride in separate train cars in "white" and "colored" compartments. When they arrived in the city they had to walk to the theater together, but separately, they also had to separate to see the movie and again to walk home. Carter states, "I don't remember even questioning the mandatory racial separation, which we accepted as breathing or waking up in Archery every morning."

From an early age, Carter proved to be an industrious student who loved reading. He attended Plains High School. Upon graduating from high school in 1941, he intended to enter the U.S. Naval Academy, but admission to this institution required the endorsement of a U.S. senator or congressman, which his father did not secure until the summer of 1942. In the meantime, he enrolled at Georgia Southwestern College in Americus and the Georgia Institute of Technology to further his preparation in science. In the summer of 1943 he entered the U.S.

Naval Academy at Annapolis, where he graduated as an ensign in 1946, 59th out of 820 students in his class, also earning a Bachelor of Science degree. In February of that same year he married Rosalynn Smith, one of his sister's best friends. Subsequently, he studied nuclear physics and reactor technology at Union College, although he did not complete his studies.

In 1948, he entered the Submarine School, was subsequently assigned to the Pacific and chosen by Admiral Hyman Rickover to participate in the then new nuclear submarine program. In 1953, although he intended to continue his career in the Navy, the death of his father led him to resign from his military duties to take over the management of the family peanut farming business in his hometown. He also showed a deep Christian sentiment from a very young age, which led him to teach Sunday school. During his political career he said that Jesus Christ had marked his life; in fact, during his presidential term he prayed several times a day.

Beginnings in politics

Member of the Georgia Senate

Jimmy Carter began his political career by serving on local boards that administered some of the schools, hospitals and libraries in his county. In 1961, he was elected to the Georgia Senate, where he served for two terms.

His 1961 election, recounted in his book *Turning Point: A Candidate, a State, and a Nation Come of Age*, was shrouded in an atmosphere of corruption led by Joe Hurst, sheriff of Quitman County. Serious irregularities occurred during the voting, including dead people voting and recounts filled with lists of people who were supposed to have come to vote in alphabetical order. In this fraudulent environment, it was a challenge to win his election. This election also marked the end of the voting system in the State of Georgia, when the U.S. Supreme Court declared unconstitutional (Gray v. Sanders ruling) in 1963 the system of *voting by county* instead of *by person*. In 1964, he was re-elected for a second two-year term. In 1966, Carter declined to run for a third re-election to begin his bid for state governor. His seat in the state senate was filled by his first cousin, Hugh Carter, elected by the Democratic Party.

Campaigns for governor

In 1966, when his term in the Georgia Senate was ending, he considered running for the U.S. House of Representatives, but when his Republican rival, Howard Callaway, withdrew his candidacy for the House to run for governor of Georgia, Carter, who did not want to see a Republican governor in his state, also withdrew from the congressional race and entered the governor's race. In the Democratic primary, Carter was the third highest vote-getter behind Ellis Arnall and Lester Maddox. Carter's participation was important and transcendent since it forced a runoff election in which Maddox, a supporter of racial segregation who had been the second most voted in the first round, won. During this process, Carter presented himself as a moderate alternative to both the more liberal Arnall and the more conservative Maddox. Although Carter was defeated, the strength of his position was seen as a success for a little-known state senator.three candidates participated in the elections: Maddox for the Democratic Party, Callaway for the Republicans and Arnal who ran as an independent. Callaway received the most votes, but Maddox was appointed governor of the state by the Georgia General Assembly.

For the next four years, Carter returned to his farm and devoted himself to carefully planning and preparing for the upcoming 1970 gubernatorial campaign. During those years, he participated in more than 1,800 political events throughout the state of Georgia.

In the 1970 election, he ran a fiercely populist Democratic primary campaign against former Governor Carl Sanders, labeling his opponent "Cufflinks Carl." Carter was never a segregationist and refused to join the segregationist *White Citizens Council*, which led to the boycott of his peanut company. His family was also one of only two to vote in favor of admitting blacks to Plains Baptist Church.However according to historian E. Stanly Godbold, during this campaign, he spoke the words segregationists wanted to hear, opposed school busing designed to encourage integration, came out in favor of private schools, and expressed a willingness to invite Alabama Governor George Wallace, known for his stance against racial integration, to give a speech on his campaign trail.In the same vein, his campaign aides released a photograph of his opponent with two black basketball players. After his narrow victory over Sanders in the primaries, Carter was elected governor by defeating the Republican candidate, Hal Suit.

After his election as governor, Carter delivered an inaugural address that deeply displeased segregationists: "I tell you in all frankness, the time for racial discrimination is over. No person, whether poor, peasant, weak, or Negro should have to bear the additional burden of being deprived of the opportunity for an education, a job, or justice."

Leroy Johnson, one of Georgia's first black state senators, reflected on this speech, stating, "We were very pleased. Many of the white segregationists were disgusted and I am convinced that those people who supported him, would not have done so if they had known he was going to make those statements."

Governor of Georgia

Carter was sworn in as Georgia's 76th governor on January 12, 1971, and served until January 14, 1975. His lieutenant governor was his predecessor, Lester Maddox, with whom he had constant public clashes during his four years in office.

Civil rights policy

As already stated, Carter declared as early as his inaugural address as governor that the era of racial segregation was over, and that discrimination had no place in the future of the state, and thus he was the first statewide public official in the so-called *Deep South* to make such a public pronouncement. During his tenure, Carter appointed quite a few African Americans to public office and was often referred to as one of the "governors of the New South." Much more moderate than his predecessors, he supported the struggle for expanded rights for African Americans and against racial segregation.

State government reforms

Carter improved government efficiency by merging some 300 state agencies down to 30. One of his aides recalled Governor Carter: "*He was right there with us, working just as hard, digging into every little problem. It was his program and he worked on it as hard as anyone and the end product was clearly his.*"

He also pushed for reforms during his legislature such as, providing equal state aid to schools in wealthy and poor areas of Georgia, creating community centers for mentally handicapped children and expanding educational programs for prisoners. Carter was especially proud of a program he introduced for the appointment of judges and state government officials based on merit rather than political influence.

Aspirations for the vice-presidency in 1972

In 1972, when George McGovern, a U.S. senator from South Dakota, ran in the Democratic primary for U.S. president, Carter called a press conference in Atlanta to warn that McGovern was ineligible, criticizing him as too liberal on both foreign and domestic policy. When McGovern's nomination was inevitable, Carter pushed to try to become his vice president. During the 1972

Democratic National Convention, he supported the candidacy of Senator Henry M. Jackson of Washington, but Carter received 30 votes in the convention's chaotic vice presidential ballot. McGovern offered second place to Reubin Askew, one of the "new southern governors," who turned it down.

Death penalty and human rights

During his presidential campaigns, he always expressed his opposition to the death penalty (as did the Democratic candidate before him, George McGovern, and the next two, Walter Mondale and Michael Dukakis). Today, Carter is known for his frontal opposition to the death penalty in all its forms, and in his Nobel Prize speech, he called for the "prohibition of the death penalty".

After the U.S. Supreme Court struck down the death penalty in the State of Georgia in 1972, Carter proposed replacing it with life imprisonment in state law (an option that had not previously existed). When the Georgia assembly passed a new death penalty law, Carter, despite expressing reservations about its constitutionality, signed the new regulations on March 28, 1973, authorizing the death penalty in cases of murder, rape, and other crimes and implementing judicial procedures that conformed to the newly announced constitutional requirements. In 1976, the Supreme Court upheld this new legislation in the murder case Coker v. Georgia, in which the Supreme

Court ruled that the death penalty was unconstitutional as applied to rape crimes.

On March 31, 1971, U.S. Army Lieutenant William Calley was sentenced to life imprisonment for the murder of 22 Vietnamese civilians in the My Lai massacre in Vietnam. President Nixon, three days after the sentencing, commuted this sentence to permanent house arrest. Jimmy Carter, dissatisfied with the life sentence, instituted *American Fighter Day by* asking Georgians to drive their cars with their lights on for a week in support of Calley. The governor of Indiana also asked that all state flags fly at half-staff in Calley's honor, and the governors of Utah and Mississippi also disagreed with the verdict.

1976 Presidential Campaign

When Carter began his bid for the U.S. presidency in 1976, he was considered a politician with little experience and little national recognition, recognized by only 2% of voters, and with little chance against more nationally known politicians. When he told his family of his intention to run for President of the United States, his mother asked him: *President of what? However,* during 1976, the Watergate scandal was still fresh in voters' minds and his position as a politician without much experience and outside the Washington D. C. politicking became an attractive factor to voters, the centerpiece of his campaign platform was government reorganization.

Democratic nomination

Carter soon became the favorite by winning the Iowa caucus and the New Hampshire primary. He used a two-pronged strategy: in the South, where the majority had tacitly embraced Alabama's George Wallace, Carter ran as a moderate favorite son. When Wallace proved to be a spent force, Carter swept the region. In the North, where Carter had little chance of winning large majorities, he appealed largely to Christian conservative voters and the rural population. He won in several Northern states, building the largest bloc. Carter's strategy was to reach a region before the other candidates could extend their influence there, he traveled more than 50,000 miles, visited 37 states and delivered more than 200 speeches before other candidates had announced they were in the race for the presidency. He refused, from the beginning, to run as a regional candidate, proving himself to be the only Democrat with a truly national strategy and thus eventually won his party's nomination.

His advance was slow; according to a Gallup poll, as late as January 26, 1976, Carter was the first choice of only four percent of Democratic voters. By mid-March, however, according to Shoup, Carter was not only well ahead of the other Democratic contenders, he was marching ahead of President Ford by a few percent.

He chose Senator Walter Mondale as his vice presidential candidate. He attacked the lack of transparency of Washington politics in his speeches, and offered a religious balm to heal the nation's wounds.

Presidential election

In his electoral campaign, Carter appealed to vague moral principles, criticized the Washington bureaucracy and promised sincerity and honesty. He framed his campaign as an "outsider," aimed at voters who were fed up with professional politicians and conventional solutions. He began the presidential campaign with a considerable lead over Ford, which narrowed over the course of the campaign, and finally allowed Carter to win on November 2, 1976, by a narrow margin. Carter won the popular vote by 50.1% to Ford's 48.0% and received 297 electoral votes to Ford's 240, becoming the first president from the so-called Deep South since the election of Zachary Taylor in 1848.

His public behavior defied established norms, during the campaign, despite his proclaimed status as a devout Christian and catechist, he gave an interview to Robert Scheer for Playboy magazine, in which he acknowledged that "I have looked at many women with lust and have committed adultery many times deep in my heart." The interview hit the newsstands a couple of weeks before the election.

Presidency of the United States (1977-1981)

Jimmy Carter was the thirty-ninth president of the United States from 1977 to 1981. Carter stood out for his relatively heterodox style, which did not fit in with the Washington establishment, nor did he have solid support from his party, and for his original opinions and judgments, without having a well-defined program.His administration tried to make a "competent and compassionate" government, but he was faced with a severe economic crisis, which made it difficult to achieve his goals, characterized by rising energy prices and stagflation. By the end of his term in office, Carter had managed to substantially reduce unemployment and the public deficit, but he was not able to completely end the recession. Carter created the Departments of Education and Energy, established a national energy policy and reformed Social Security. In foreign affairs, Carter initiated the Camp David Accords, the Panama Canal treaties and the second round of the SALT Agreements. Throughout his tenure as president, Carter strongly emphasized human rights. He returned the Panama Canal Zone to Panama, facing criticism at home for his decision, which was seen as another sign of U.S. weakness and its habit of backing down in the face of confrontation. The last year of his presidential term was marked by several major crises, such as the 1979 seizure of the US embassy in Iran and hostage-taking by Iranian students, the unsuccessful attempt to rescue the hostages, a severe fuel shortage and the beginning of the Afghan War.

Inauguration

In his inauguration speech he said:

Carter had campaigned on a promise to eliminate the shenanigans of the so-called "*imperial presidency*" that prevailed under Richard Nixon and he began his presidency, in keeping with that promise, on the day of his inauguration; walking down Pennsylvania Avenue from the Capitol to the White House in his inaugural parade, breaking with protocol and recent history. His first steps in the White House went further in this direction, cutting the staff of advisors by a third, eliminating drivers for cabinet members and putting the presidential yacht, the USS Sequoia, up for sale.

Domestic policy

On Carter's first day in office, January 20, 1977, he fulfilled a campaign promise by issuing an Executive Order declaring unconditional amnesty for Vietnam War draft dodgers.

Under Carter's tutelage, the Airline Deregulation Act of 1978 was passed, which eliminated the Civil Aeronautics Board, and also pushed for deregulation of trucking, railroads, communications, finance and industry.

Among presidents who have served at least one full term as president, Carter is the only one who did not make any Supreme Court appointments.

Carter was the first president to set out to address the issue of gay rights. He opposed the Briggs Initiative, a California bill that banned homosexuals and gay rights advocates from being public school teachers. The Carter administration was the first to meet with a group of gay rights activists and in recent years acted in favor of civil unions and ended the ban on homosexuals in the military. in this regard he stated that he "*opposes all forms of discrimination on the basis of sexual orientation and believes there should be equal protection under the law for people who differ in sexual orientation*."

Budget

Despite calling for reform of the tax system during his presidential campaign, when he came to power he did little to change it.

During all years of the presidency there was a deficit in the federal government's budget, although the percentage of debt to GDP decreased slightly. His Alaska Lands National Interest Conservation Act converted 103 million acres (417,000 km^2) into a national park in Alaska.

Relations with Congress

Carter ran a successful election campaign defining himself as a "Washington outsider," in which he criticized President Gerald Ford and the Democrat-controlled U.S. Congress. As president, he continued this line, his refusal to play by "Washington rules" contributing to the Carter administration's difficult relationship with Congress. Hamilton Jordan and Frank Moore, in particular, clashed early on, with Democratic leaders, such as House Speaker Tip O'Neill. Relations with Capitol Hill soured over unreturned phone calls, insults (both real and imagined) and an unwillingness to trade political favors and weakened the president's ability to push his ambitious agenda.

During the first 100 days of his presidency, Carter sent a letter to Congress, proposing the rejection of several bills. Among those who voiced opposition to that proposal was Senator Russell B. Long, a powerful Democrat on the Senate Finance Committee. Carter's plan was rejected, producing a sense of bitterness in the Carter administration.

The rejection drove a wedge between the White House and Congress, Carter said that the most intense and growing opposition to his policies came from the liberal wing of the Democratic Party itself, which he attributed to Ted Kennedy's ambition to replace him as president.

A few months into his term, and thinking he had the support of about 74 congressmen, Carter issued a "blacklist" of 19 bills that Carter said were a "pork barrel" of government spending, stating that he would veto any legislative initiative that included any bill on this list.

This list met with opposition from the leader of the Democratic party. Carter had included a rivers and harbors bill as unnecessary, and House Speaker Tip O'Neill thought it inadvisable for the president to interfere in matters that had traditionally been part of Congress's purview. After these events, Carter was further weakened and had to sign a bill containing projects on his blacklist.

Later, Congress refused to pass major provisions of his consumer protection law and his labor reform package, and Carter vetoed a public works package as "inflationary" because it contained what he considered unnecessary spending. Congressional leaders perceived that public support for Carter's legislative initiative was weak, and they took advantage of it. After gutting the consumer protection bill, they transformed his tax plan into nothing more than special interest spending, after which Carter referred to the Congressional Tax Committee as a "wolf pack."

Oil crisis

In 1973, during the Nixon administration, the Organization of Petroleum Exporting Countries (OPEC) reduced the supplies of oil available on the world market, partly due to the depreciation of the dollar caused by Nixon's departure from the gold standard and partly as a reaction against the United States for sending arms to Israel during the Yom Kippur War. This triggered the 1973 oil crisis which meant a sharp rise in oil prices that pushed up inflation and slowed growth. The U.S. government, following the announcement, imposed price controls on gasoline and oil, which led to shortages and long lines at gas stations. The lines were avoided by removing price controls on gasoline; these oil controls remained in place until the Reagan presidency. When Carter came to the White House in 1977, he told Americans that the energy crisis was *a clear and present danger to the nation* and *the moral equivalent of war*, and he devised a plan to try to deal with the problem, stating that the world's oil supply could probably only meet U.S. demand for six to eight more years.

In 1977, Carter convinced Democrats in Congress to create the U.S. Department of Energy to promote energy conservation. Carter established price controls on oil and natural gas and installed solar panels to heat domestic hot water in the White House and installed a wood-burning stove in his home. He ordered the General Services Administration to shut off hot water at some federal facilities, and called for public Christmas decorations to remain unlit for Christmas 1979 and 1980. Controls were set nationwide on thermostats in government and commercial buildings so that they would not exceed temperatures in the winter above 18.33 °C or fall below 25 °C in the summer.

In reaction to the energy crisis and growing concerns about air pollution, Carter also signed into law the National Energy Act and the Public Utility Regulatory Policy Act. The purpose of these laws was to encourage energy conservation and the development of domestic energy resources, including renewables such as solar and wind power.

However, during the 1979 crisis, Carter reinstated some price controls on gasoline, which again caused queues at gas stations. During his "malaise" speech, he announced a gradual liberalization of price controls, along with the imposition of a "Windfall Profits Tax" to fund energy efficiency initiatives. The tax was introduced in 1980 by taxing domestic oil production; the tax was repealed in 1988, when prices collapsed, making it possible to abolish the tax. This tax was not a levy on profits, but an excise tax on the difference between a base price and the market price.

Economics: stagflation and the appointment of Paul Volcker

The economic history of the Carter Administration can be divided into two roughly equal periods. The first two years were a time of continued recovery from the severe recession of 1973-1975, which had left fixed capital investment at its lowest level since the 1970 recession and unemployment at 9%. The other two years were marked by double-digit inflation with very high interest rates, oil shortages, and low economic growth. The nation's economy grew at an average of 3.4% during the Carter Administration (on par with the historical average). Each of these two-year periods, however, differed radically.

The U.S. economy, which had grown by 5% in 1976, continued at a similar pace during 1977 and 1978. Unemployment declined from 7.5% in January 1977 to 5.6% in May 1979, with more than 9 million net new jobs created during that interval, and per capita household income grew by 5% between 1976 and 1978. The recovery in business investment in evidence during 1976 also strengthened. Private fixed investment (machinery and construction) grew by 30% from 1976 to 1979, housing sales and construction grew likewise in 1978, and industrial production, vehicle production and sales grew by nearly 15%, with the exception of new housing starts, which remained slightly below their 1972 peak, each of these benchmarks reached record levels in 1978 or 1979.

The energy crisis of 1979 ended this period of growth, inflation and interest rates remained high, while economic growth, job creation and consumer confidence declined sharply. The relatively loose monetary policy adopted by Federal Reserve Chairman William G. Miller had contributed to the generation of somewhat higher inflation, with increases from 5.8% in 1976 to 7.7% in 1978. OPEC's sharp and sudden rise in crude oil prices drove inflation to double-digit levels, averaging 11.3% in 1979 and 13.5% in 1980. The sudden gasoline shortage at the beginning of the 1979 vacation season exacerbated the problem, and would come to symbolize the crisis among the general public. The shortage, which originated in the closure of the Amerada Hess refining facilities, led to a lawsuit by the federal government against the company.

Carter, like his predecessor President Ford, asked Congress to impose controls on energy prices, medical products, and consumer prices, but was unable to get these measures passed because of strong congressional opposition, but using an Energy Conservation and Policy Act, passed by Congress during Gerald Ford's presidency, which gave presidents the authority to deregulate oil prices in the U.S. market, he succeeded in encouraging oil production and savings.Oil imports, which had reached a record 2.4 billion barrels in 1977 (fifty percent of U.S. supply), were cut in half between 1979 and 1983.

In 1987 journalist William Greider wrote *The Secrets of the Temple*, a book published shortly after the stock market crash, in which he states that Volcker and his subsequent protégés have subsequently dominated the Federal Reserve for at least several decades through several U.S. administrations During the Carter administration, the economy suffered from double-digit inflation, along with very high interest rates, oil shortages, high unemployment and sluggish economic growth. Productivity growth in the United States had slowed to an average annual rate of 1%, down from 3.2% in the 1960s. There was also a growing federal budget deficit, which increased to $66 billion. The 1970s is described as a period of stagflation, as well as higher interest rates. Price inflation (a rise in the general price level) created uncertainty in budgeting and planning and made strikes for pay raises more likely. Carter, like Nixon, asked Congress to impose price controls on energy, medicine, and consumer prices, but Congress disagreed.

Following a cabinet reshuffle, Carter appointed G. William Miller as Secretary of the Treasury, who until then had served as Chairman of the Federal Reserve. To replace him and in order to calm the markets, Carter appointed Paul Volcker as the new chairman of the Fed. Volcker pursued a tight monetary policy to lower inflation. Volcker and Carter succeeded, but only after first going through a recessionary phase during which the economy slowed and unemployment rose. The easing of inflation saw results during the first term of Ronald Reagan, who reappointed Volcker as chairman of the Fed.

Under Volcker's leadership, the Federal Reserve raised the discount rate from 10% when he took office in August 1979 to 12% within two months. The prime rate reached 21.5% in December 1980, the highest in U.S. history. Carter enacted an austerity program that he tried to justify because inflation had reached "a state of crisis," inflation and the short-term interest rate reached eighteen percent in February and March 1980. Fixed income investments (bonds, both held by Wall Street and pensions paid to retirees) were worth less and less. High interest rates led to a severe recession in the 1980s, which coincided with the campaign for reelection.

Discourse of "discomfort".

In 1979, when the oil crisis began, Carter was planning to give his fifth major speech on energy, yet he felt the American people were no longer listening. Carter retreated to the presidential residence at Camp David. For more than a week, a veil of secrecy shrouded his proceedings, he summoned dozens of prominent Democratic Party leaders, members of Congress, governors, labor leaders, academics and members of the clergy to his residence. His analyst, Pat Caddell, told him that the American people were facing a crisis of confidence prompted by the assassinations of John F. Kennedy, Robert F. Kennedy and Martin Luther King, Jr; the Vietnam War; and the Watergate Scandal. On July 15, 1979, Carter gave a nationally televised speech in which he identified what he believed to be a "crisis of confidence" among the American people. This became known as his "malaise speech," although the word never appeared in the speech.

The speech was written by Hendrik Hertzberg and Gordon Stewart. Although it has often been said to have been poorly received, The New York Times ran the following headline a week later "Speech Boosts Carter's Rating to 37%, Public Feels OK with Crisis of Confidence, Tugged at the heartstrings.

Carter's subsequent reelection loss prompted other politicians to rule out soliciting energy savings from Americans in a similar manner. Three days after the speech, Carter asked for the resignation of all members of his Cabinet, ultimately accepting the resignations of the five who had clashed with the White House at the top, including Energy Secretary James Schlesinger and Health, Education and Welfare Chief Joseph A. Califano, known as a supporter of Senator Ted Kennedy. Carter later admitted in his memoirs that he simply should have asked for the resignation of only the five members who resigned. In 2008, a U.S. News and World Report report stated:

"After campaigning that he would never appoint a Chief of Staff, Carter appointed Jordan as a new White House Chief of Staff. Many in the administration chafed when Jordan circulated a "questionnaire" that read more like a loyalty oath. "I think the idea was that they were going to firm up the administration, show that there was real change by these personnel changes, and move on," remembers Mondale. "But the message the American people got was that we were falling apart." Carter later admitted in his memoirs that he should simply have asked only those five members for their resignations. In 2008, a U.S. News and World Report piece stated":

"After a campaign [in which he promised] he would never again appoint a chief of staff, Carter named Jordan White House chief of staff. Many in the administration were irritated when Jordan circulated a "questionnaire" that looked more like a loyalty oath. "I think the idea was that they were going to concretize the administration, showing that there was real change from these staff changes, and move on," Mondale recalls. "But the message the American people got was that they were going down." Carter later admitted in his memoir that he should only have asked for the resignation of those five members. In 2008, a U.S. News and World Report piece stated."

Foreign policy

South Korea

During his first month in office, Carter decreased the defense budget by six billion dollars. One of his first acts was to order the unilateral withdrawal of all nuclear weapons from South Korea and to announce his intention to reduce the number of U.S. troops stationed in that country. Some military officials criticized this decision in private conversations and in testimony before congressional committees, in 1977, General John K. Singlaub, chief of staff of U.S. forces in South Korea, publicly criticized Carter's decision to reduce the number of troops stationed there. On March 21, 1977, Carter relieved him of his post, stating that his publicly stated views were "incompatible with the announced national security policy".

Carter had planned to withdraw all but 14,000 U.S. Air Force troops and logistics specialists in 1982, but in 1978, after cutting only 3,600 troops, he was forced to abandon the project under pressure from Congress and opposition from his generals.

Camp David Agreements

Carter Cabinet Secretary of State Cyrus Vance and National Security Advisor Zbigniew Brzezinski paid close attention to the Arab-Israeli conflict. Diplomatic communications between Israel and Egypt increased significantly after the 1973 Yom Kippur War and the Carter administration believed that the time was right for a comprehensive settlement of the conflict.

In mid-1978, Carter was very concerned, as the Separation Treaty between Egypt and Israel had expired only a few months earlier. Carter decided to send a special envoy to the Middle East. The U.S. ambassador shuttled back and forth between Cairo (Egypt) and Tel Aviv trying to narrow the differences between the two countries. It was then suggested that the foreign ministers meet at Leeds Castle (England) to discuss the possibilities of peace. They tried to reach an agreement, but the foreign ministers failed to do so. Subsequently, the 1978 Camp David Accords were reached, one of Carter's most important achievements during his presidency.

The accords were a peace agreement between Israel and Egypt negotiated by Carter, which culminated earlier negotiations in the Middle East. In these negotiations King Hassan II of Morocco acted as a negotiator between Arab interests in Israel, and Nicolae Ceausescu of Romania acted as an intermediary between Israel and the Palestine

Liberation Organization. When the initial negotiations ended, Egyptian President Anwar Sadat approached Carter for help. Carter invited Israeli Prime Minister Menachem Beguin and Anwar el-Sadat to Camp David to continue negotiations. They arrived on August 8, 1978, neither leader having met since the Vienna meeting. President Carter acted as mediator between the two leaders and spoke with each separately to try to reach an agreement. After a month had passed without any resolution, President Carter decided to meet with both leaders during a trip to Gettysburg, Pennsylvania to break the impasse. There he showed them the site of an American Civil War battle, explained the history of the battle and emphasized how important it was to achieve peace in order to bring prosperity to the people. A lesson that contributed to the fact that when Beguin and Sadat returned to Camp David, they understood that they had to sign some kind of agreement.

On September 12, 1978, President Carter suggested dividing the Peace Treaty negotiations into two frameworks: Framework 1 would deal with the West Bank and Gaza Strip, while Framework 2 would deal with the Sinai.

- The first framework dealt with the Palestinian territories of the West Bank and Gaza Strip.

- The first point concerned the election of a self-government, which would allow full autonomy to the inhabitants of both territories. This government would be elected by the Palestinians and would only deal with municipal affairs.
- The second step would be the granting of autonomy to the Palestinians, especially in municipal affairs.

It was expected that after these steps, the State of Palestine could be negotiated.

Framework 1 was not very well received by Palestinians and Jordanians who objected to the fact that Beguin and Sadat made decisions about their ultimate fate, without consulting them or their leaders.

- The second framework would deal with the Sinai Peninsula. It consisted of two points:
-
    - The two parties, Egypt and Israel, should negotiate a treaty within six months based on the principle of Egyptian sovereignty over the Sinai Peninsula and Israel's withdrawal from that region.

- This treaty would be followed by the establishment of diplomatic, political, economic, and cultural relations between Egypt and Israel.

President Carter admitted that despite everything, "there were still great difficulties and many difficult issues to resolve.

The reaction to this proposal in the Arab world was very negative. In November 1978, an emergency meeting convened by the Arab League was held in Damascus. Once again, Egypt was the main topic of the meeting, and the treaty proposal that Egypt was to sign was condemned. Sadat was also attacked by the Arab press for breaking ranks with the Arab League and having betrayed the Arab world. Discussions concerning the future peace treaty were held in both countries. Israel insisted during the negotiations that the treaty with Egypt should supersede all of Egypt's other treaties, including those signed with the Arab League and Arab countries. Israel also wanted access to the oil discovered in the Sinai region. President Carter intervened and informed the Israelis that the United States would provide Israel with the oil supply it needed for the next 15 years, if Egypt decided not to provide it to Israel.

The Israeli parliament approved the treaty with a comfortable majority. On the other hand, the Egyptian government was arguing about different issues. They did not like the fact that the proposed treaty would supersede all other treaties. Moreover, the Egyptians were disappointed that they had not succeeded in linking the Sinai issue to the Palestine problem.

On March 26, 1979, Egypt and Israel signed the peace treaty in Washington D. C., Carter's role was essential. Aaron David Miller interviewed many officials in his book *The Much Too Promised Land* (2008) and concluded the following: *No matter who you ask, Americans, Egyptians, or Israelis, most agree: without Carter there would have been no peace treaty*.

Human rights

Carter initially departed from the established policy of containment toward the Soviet Union. He promoted a foreign policy that placed human rights among his priorities, a break with the attitude of his predecessors who paid no attention to human rights abuses committed by countries allied with the U.S. The Carter Administration stopped supporting the historically U.S.-backed Somoza regime in Nicaragua and gave aid to the new Sandinista National Liberation Front government that took power after the overthrow of Somoza. However, Carter ignored a request from Archbishop Oscar Romero in El Salvador not to send military aid to that country. Romero was later assassinated for his criticism of human rights violations in

El Salvador. Carter was also criticized by feminist activist Andrea Dworkin for disregarding women's rights in Saudi Arabia.

Carter continued his predecessors' policy of imposing sanctions on Rhodesia, and after Bishop Abel Muzorewa was elected prime minister, he protested the exclusion of Robert Mugabe and Joshua Nkomo from the elections. Strong pressure from the United States and the United Kingdom brought about new elections in Rhodesia (now Zimbabwe), which led to the election of Robert Mugabe as prime minister; after which, sanctions were lifted, and the country was granted diplomatic recognition. Carter was also known for his criticism of Alfredo Stroessner of Paraguay and Augusto Pinochet of Chile, although both Stroessner and Pinochet attended the signing of the Panama Canal Treaty, he also protested against *Apartheid* in South Africa.

People's Republic of China

Carter continued Richard Nixon's policy of normalizing relations with the People's Republic of China. National Security Advisor Zbigniew Brzezinski and Michel Oksenberg traveled to Beijing in early 1978, where together with Leonard Woodcock, Director of the Liaison Office, they laid the groundwork for an agreement to achieve full diplomatic and commercial relations with the People's Republic of China. In the Joint Communiqué on the Establishment of Diplomatic Relations of January 1, 1979, the United States transferred diplomatic recognition of Taipei to Beijing and reiterated the *Shanghai Communiqué* which recognized the existence of a single China and acknowledged that Taiwan was part of it. Beijing, for its part, accepted that the United States would continue to maintain trade, cultural relations and unofficial contacts with Taiwan. The United States continued to maintain contacts with Taiwan under the Taiwan Relations Act.

Panama Canal Treaties

One of the most controversial moments of Carter's presidency was the negotiation and signing of the Panama Canal Treaties in September 1977. These treaties, which essentially involved the transfer of the Canal from the Americans to the Republic of Panama, were rejected by the Republican Party, arguing that a U.S. settlement of great strategic value was being transferred to an unstable and corrupt country led by General Omar Torrijos, who had not been democratically elected. Those who supported the treaties, on the contrary, defended that the canal had been built within Panamanian territory and that therefore, the United States through its control had occupied part of another country, so that the agreement was intended to return to Panama full sovereignty over its territory. Following the signing of the Canal Treaties in

June 1978, Carter visited Panama with his wife and twelve U.S. Senators, in the midst of widespread student unrest against the Torrijos government. Carter later urged the Torrijos regime to curb its dictatorial policies and move gradually toward democracy in Panama.

SALT II

One of the keys to Carter's foreign policy, which involved a great deal of hard work, was the signing of the SALT II Treaty (Strategic Arms Limitation Talks), which reduced the number of nuclear weapons produced or maintained by both the United States and the Soviet Union. The work of Gerald Ford and Richard Nixon had led to SALT I, which reduced the number of nuclear weapons produced, but Carter wanted to go further in reducing nuclear weapons. Carter's main goal, as he stated in his inaugural address, was the complete disappearance of nuclear weapons from the world.

To this end, Carter and the leader of the Soviet Union, Leonid Brezhnev, reached agreement on the SALT II Treaty in 1979. However, Congress refused to ratify it, as many believed that signing the treaties would weaken U.S. defenses. After the Soviet intervention in Afghanistan in late 1979, Carter withdrew the treaty from congressional consideration and it was never ratified, although it was signed by Carter and Brezhnev. Even so, both powers honored the commitments set forth in the negotiations signed by the two dignitaries.

Intervention in Afghanistan

Jimmy Carter was shocked by the Soviet intervention in Afghanistan in December 1979 and quickly took action, including arming the mujahideen. Vice President Walter Mondale publicly expressed his disapproval of the aggressive policy the Soviet Union had adopted.

The Soviets had held previous talks with the Afghan leadership that seemed to indicate that they did not intend to intervene, yet the Politburo, with much hesitation, had seriously considered the possibility of military action. It has been argued that U.S. financial aid to Afghan dissidents, which included Islamists and other Afghan mujahideen militants, and the Soviet desire to protect the leftist Afghan government, were the factors that ultimately convinced the Soviets to intervene.

On the other hand, seeking to destabilize the area, the CIA since the early 1970s together with the British supported the Afghan mujahideen militants and in 1975 had participated in a failed attempt at civil war, organized from Pakistan, which was a resounding failure; it provided money and weapons to the fundamentalist insurgents through Inter-Services Intelligence (ISI) (Pakistan's secret services, in a program called Operation Cyclone.

The US began secretly sending limited financial aid to Afghan Islamist factions on July 3, 1978. In December 1979 the USSR overthrew Prime Minister Hafizullah Amin, whom it accused of being a CIA agent and who had previously staged a coup against the legitimate government of Nur Taraki. U.S. politicians, both Republicans and Democrats, said that the Soviets were positioning themselves to dominate Middle East oil. Others believed that the Soviet Union feared that the revolution and Islamization of Afghanistan would spread to the Muslim population of the USSR.

After the overthrow of Amin, Carter announced what is known as the Carter Doctrine, consisting of the US commitment to use force if necessary to gain access to the oil resources of the Persian Gulf. The increase in tension between the blocs caused by this doctrine culminated in the boycott of the 1980 Moscow Olympic Games, to which the USSR and its allies would respond with their absence at the Los Angeles Games in 1984.

The Russian Wheat Treaty, which was intended to establish trade with the USSR and ease Cold War tensions, was also terminated. Grain exports had been beneficial to farmers, and Carter's embargo marked the beginning of difficulties for U.S. farmers.

Carter and Brzezinski initiated a covert program of training the mujahideen in Pakistan and Afghanistan in order to thwart Soviet plans. Carter's diplomatic policies toward Pakistan changed dramatically. The administration had cut off financial aid to the country in early 1979 when religious fundamentalists, encouraged by the tide of Islamic military dictatorship in Pakistan, burned the U.S. Embassy there. International involvement in Pakistan increased considerably with the Soviet intervention. The then President of Pakistan, General Muhammad Zia-ul-Haq, was offered $400 million to subsidize the anti-communist mujahideen in Afghanistan. General Zia declined the offer as insufficient and the U.S. was forced to increase aid to Pakistan.

Reagan subsequently greatly expanded this program. Critics of this policy blamed Carter and Reagan for the instability of Afghanistan's post-Soviet governments, which led to the rise of an Islamic theocracy in the region.

Iran hostage crisis

The main U.S. conflict over human rights came as a result of Carter's relations with the Shah of Iran. Shah Mohammad Reza Pahlavi, had been a strong ally of the United States since World War II and one of the so-called "twin pillars" on which U.S. strategic policy in the Middle East was based, (the other being Saudi Arabia). However, the sah had exercised a strongly autocratic rule, which was seen as defiantly kleptocratic at home. In 1953 he organized, together with the Eisenhower administration, a coup d'état to remove the elected prime minister, Mohammed Mossadegh.

On a state visit to Iran during 1978, Carter spoke publicly in favor of the Shah, calling him a *"leader of supreme wisdom"* and a pillar of stability in the volatile Middle East, in a speech that was never broadcast on U.S. television. When the Iranian Revolution broke out shortly thereafter and the sah was overthrown, the United States did not intervene directly and the sah had to march into permanent exile, in January 1979. Carter initially denied him entry to the United States, even on grounds of medical urgency.

Despite his initial refusal to allow Shah to enter the United States, on October 22, 1979, Carter granted him entry clearance and temporary asylum for the duration of his cancer treatment, Shah returned to Panama on December 15, 1979. However, in November of that same year, in response to the sah's entry into the U.S., Iranian militants seized the U.S. embassy in Tehran, holding 52 Americans hostage. The Iranians demanded their release in exchange:

- The sah's return to Iran for trial.
- The return to the Iranian people of the wealth accumulated by the sah.

- Acknowledgement of U.S. culpability for its past actions in Iran, and a request for an apology.
- U.S. pledge not to interfere in Iran's affairs in the future.

Although that same year, the Shah left the United States, he would die in Egypt in 1980. The hostage crisis continued and dominated the last year of Carter's presidency. The subsequent response to the crisis - from the "Rose Garden" strategy of staying inside the White House, to the failed attempt to rescue the hostages by military means (Operation Eagle Claw), were largely responsible for Carter's electoral defeat in the 1980 presidential election. On November 14, 1979, after the hostages were taken, Carter issued Executive Order 12170, which blocked Iranian government property, freezing Iranian government bank accounts in U.S. banks totaling $8 billion U.S. dollars at the time. These embargoes were used as a bargaining chip for the release of the hostages.

In the days before Ronald Reagan assumed the U.S. presidency following his election victory, Algerian diplomat Abdulkarim Ghuraib had initiated negotiations between the United States and Iran, which culminated in the "Algiers Accords" of January 19, 1981, just one day before the end of Carter's presidency. The agreements involved Iran's commitment to release the hostages immediately. In addition, Executive Orders 12277 and 12,285, issued by Carter, involved the release of all property belonging to the Iranian government and all assets belonging to the sah that were in the United States, as well as a guarantee that the hostages would not pursue any legal claims against the Iranian government in connection with the kidnapping. Iran also agreed to place $100 billion of the frozen assets in an escrow account, with Iran and the United States agreeing to set up a tribunal to settle claims by U.S. citizens for losses incurred by the Iranian government. This tribunal, known as the Iran-US Claims Tribunal, would award more than two billion dollars to US claimants and has been described as one of the most important arbitration bodies in the history of international law.

Although the release of the hostages was negotiated and guaranteed by the Carter administration, the hostages were not released until January 20, 1981, moments after Reagan had been inaugurated as president.

1980 Elections

At the end of 1979, a year before the elections, Carter was far behind in the public's preferences, and even political observers thought that he could be replaced by Edward Kennedy as the Democratic Party's candidate. However, events on the international scene, such as the taking of the Iranian embassy hostages and the Russian invasion of Afghanistan improved his position in the polls and pushed him far enough to win his party's nomination. The subsequent failure of the hostage rescue once again dented his image for re-election.

Carter lost the election to Republican Ronald Reagan. The breakdown of votes was 43.9 million, representing 50.7% of the total, for Reagan and 35.5 million votes, representing 41%, for Carter. Independent candidate John B. Anderson received 5.7 million votes, 6.6% of the total. However, the fact that Carter's support was not concentrated in a particular geographic region caused Reagan to win a very clear 91% of the pledges, leaving Carter with only six states and the District of Columbia. Reagan won a total of 489 electoral votes to Carter's 49.

Carter's defeat marked the first time a sitting president had failed to win a second term since Herbert Hoover's presidency in 1932. Carter was able to fulfill his promise of the live release of the 52 hostages at the U.S. embassy in Iran, but failed to secure their release before the election. Carter ultimately negotiated their release, although Iran did not agree to their release until minutes after Ronald Reagan took office as president. In recognition of his intervention, Reagan asked him to go to West Germany to receive the hostages after their release.

During the campaign, Carter was mocked for the so-called rabbit incident, an encounter with a swamp rabbit while fishing on April 20, 1979.

Post-presidency

In 1981, Carter returned to peanut farming in Georgia, which he had placed in a blind trust during his presidency to avoid even the appearance of conflict of interest. He found that the trustees had mismanaged the business, leaving him more than $1 million in debt. In the years since, he has led an active life, founding the Carter Center, building his presidential library, teaching at Emory University in Atlanta, and publishing several books.

Legacy

Upon leaving office, his presidency was assessed by most as a failure. In the historical ranking of U.S. presidents, Carter's presidency has ranged from 19th to 34th. While Carter's presidency received mixed reviews from some historians, his fight for peace above all else and his humanitarian efforts since leaving office have led him to be widely recognized as one of the most successful former presidents in U.S. history.

Jimmy Carter and his vice president Walter Mondale have been the longest-lived post-presidency team in American history. On December 11, 2006, they completed 25 years and 325 days since leaving office, surpassing the previous record set by President John Adams and Thomas Jefferson as vice president, who died on July 4, 1826. In August 2012, he surpassed Herbert Hoover as the president who has lived the longest since his term ended.

Jimmy Carter is one of only four presidents, and the only one in modern U.S. history, who did not have the opportunity to appoint a justice to the Supreme Court.

Public image

The *Independent* newspaper published:

Carter began his term with a 66% approval rating, but this dropped to 34% by the time he left office, with 55% disapproval.

Polls early in the 1976 presidential campaign suggested that many did not forgive Gerald Ford for his relationship with Richard Nixon and the Watergate scandal. Carter, by comparison, seemed an honest, sincere and well-meaning Southerner.

This situation changed when Carter ran for reelection, when Ronald Reagan's self-confidence contrasted with Carter's serious, introspective temperament. Carter's personal attention to detail and his apparent indecisiveness and weakness were accentuated by Reagan's charm with voters. Carter's personal attention to detail and his apparent indecisiveness and weakness were accentuated by Reagan's charm with voters. Ultimately, the combination of economic problems, the Iran hostage crisis, and Washington's lack of cooperation made it easy for Reagan to portray Carter as an ineffective leader.

Since leaving office, Carter's reputation has greatly improved. Carter's presidential approval rating, which peaked at 31% just before the 1980 election, was at 64% in early 2009. Carter's post-presidency has also been favorably received. Carter explains that a large part of this change was due to Reagan's successor, George HW Bush, who actively sought him out and was much friendlier and more interested in his advice than Reagan had been. Carter has maintained working relationships with former Presidents George H.W. Bush, Bill Clinton and George W. Bush. Bush, Bill Clinton and George W. Bush, and despite their political differences, the three have become good friends over the years working together on various humanitarian projects.

Carter Center

As president, Carter expressed his goal of making a government that was "competent and compassionate." In pursuit of that vision, he has been involved in a variety of domestic and international public policy, conflict resolution, human rights and charitable causes.

In 1982, he founded The Carter Center in Atlanta to promote human rights and alleviate unnecessary human suffering. This non-profit, non-governmental institution promotes democracy, seeks mediation and conflict prevention, and monitors the electoral process in support of free and fair elections. In addition, it works to improve global health through the control and eradication of diseases such as Dracunculiasis, onchocerciasis, malaria, trachoma, lymphatic filariasis and schistosomiasis. It also strives to decrease the stigma of mental illness and improve nutrition by increasing crop production in Africa. A major achievement of the Center has been the elimination of more than 99% of cases of Guinea worm disease, a debilitating parasite that has existed since ancient times, from an estimated 3.5 million cases in 1986 to fewer than 10,000 in 2007. The Carter Center has overseen 70 elections in 28 countries since 1989. It has worked to resolve conflicts in Haiti, Bosnia, Ethiopia, North Korea, Sudan, Venezuela and other countries. The Carter Center actively supports human rights defenders around the world and has intervened with heads of state on their behalf.

Nobel Peace Prize

In 2002, former President Carter received the Nobel Peace Prize for his work to find peaceful solutions to international conflicts, promote democracy, human rights and economic and social development through the Carter Center. Three presidents, Theodore Roosevelt, Woodrow Wilson and Barack Obama, have received the award during their presidencies, Carter is unique in receiving the award for his actions after leaving office. He is, along with Martin Luther King, Jr. one of two native Georgians to receive the Nobel.

Diplomacy

North Korea

In 1994, North Korea had expelled researchers from the International Atomic Energy Agency and threatened to begin processing spent nuclear fuel. In response, then-President Bill Clinton pushed for sanctions and ordered large numbers of troops and vehicles to the area to prepare for war.

Clinton secretly recruited Carter to carry out a peace mission in North Korea under the guise of Carter's private mission, Clinton saw in Carter a way to get North Korean President Kim Il-sung to back down without breaking his reputation.

Carter negotiated an agreement with Kim Il-sung, but went further and also engineered a treaty, which he announced on CNN, without White House authorization, as a way to force the United States into action. The Clinton Administration signed a later version of the Agreed Framework, under which North Korea agreed to freeze and eventually dismantle its nuclear program and comply with its nonproliferation obligations, in exchange for oil deliveries, the construction of two light water reactors to replace its graphite reactors, and discussions for the eventual establishment of diplomatic relations.

The agreement was hailed at the time as a major diplomatic achievement. However, in December 2002, the Framework Agreements collapsed as a result of a dispute between the George W. Bush administration and the North Korean government of Kim Jong-il. In 2001, President George W. Bush had decided to adopt a confrontational stance towards North Korea and in January 2002, he included North Korea as part of an "axis of evil". In the meantime, North Korea began to develop uranium enrichment capabilities. Bush and other U.S. Administration opponents of the Framework Agreements believed that the North Korean government was never willing to give up its nuclear weapons program; on the contrary, supporters of the agreement believed that it might have been a success and that it was undermined.

Middle East

Carter and Carter Center experts attended unofficial negotiations between Israelis and Palestinians to design a model peace agreement, called the Geneva Accord, in 2002-2003. Carter has also in recent years become a frequent critic of Israel's policies in Lebanon, the West Bank and Gaza.

In April 2008, the London-based Arabic newspaper, Al-Hayat, reported that Carter met with Hamas leader Khaled Mashaal on his visit to Syria. The Carter Center initially neither confirmed nor denied the story. The U.S.

State Department considers Hamas to be a terrorist organization. On this Middle East trip, Carter also placed a wreath at the tomb of Yasser Arafat in Ramallah on April 14, 2008. Carter said on April 23 that neither Condoleezza Rice nor anyone at the State Department had warned him not to meet with Hamas leaders during his trip. Carter discussed with Mashaal regarding several issues, including "prisoner exchange formulas to obtain the release of Corporal Shalit."

In May 2007, while arguing that the United States should speak directly to Iran, Carter claimed that Israel had 150 nuclear weapons in its arsenal.

In December 2008, Carter visited Damascus again, where he met with Syrian President Bashar Assad and the leader of Hamas. During his visit, he gave an exclusive interview to "Adelante" magazine, the first successful interview for any U.S. president, current or former, with Syrian media.

Africa

Carter held summits in Egypt and Tunisia in 1995-1996 to address violence in the Great Lakes region of Africa and played a key role in negotiating the 1999 Nairobi Agreement between Sudan and Uganda.

On July 18, 2007, Carter met with Nelson Mandela in Johannesburg, South Africa, to announce his involvement in a new humanitarian organization called the Global

Elders. In October 2007, Carter visited Darfur with several of the Global Elders members, including Desmond Tutu. Sudanese security prevented him from visiting a Darfur tribal leader, which led to a heated argument.

On June 18, 2007, Carter, accompanied by his wife, arrived in Dublin, Ireland, for talks with President Mary McAleese and Bertie Ahern on human rights issues. On June 19, Carter attended and spoke at the annual Human Rights Forum in Croke Park. An agreement between Irish Aid and The Carter Center was also signed on this day.

In November 2008, Carter, former United Nations Secretary General Kofi Annan, and Graca Machel, wife of Nelson Mandela, attempted to enter Zimbabwe to inspect the human rights situation, but were prevented from doing so by the government of President Robert Mugabe.

Latin America

Carter led a mission to Haiti in 1994 with Senator Sam Nunn and former Chairman of the U.S. Joint Chiefs of Staff General Colin Powell to prevent a U.S.-led multinational invasion and restore democratically elected Haitian President Jean-Bertrand Aristide to power.

Carter visited Cuba in May 2002 and held talks with Fidel Castro and the Cuban government. He was allowed to address the public uncensored on Cuban national television and radio, with a speech he wrote and delivered in Spanish. In the speech, he called on the United States to end "a 43-year-old ineffective economic embargo" and on Castro to hold free elections, improve human rights, and allow more civil liberties. He met with political dissidents, visited an AIDS hospital, a medical school, a biotechnology center, an agricultural production cooperative, and a school for disabled children, and threw out an honorary pitch at a baseball game in Havana. Carter's visit marked the first visit to the island since the 1959 Cuban Revolution by a U.S. president, in or out of office.

Carter visited Venezuela's elections as an observer on August 15, 2004. European Union observers had refused to participate, claiming that the government of Hugo Chávez imposed too many restrictions on them. The Carter Center declared that the process "suffered numerous irregularities", but said it did not observe or receive "evidence of fraud that would have changed the outcome of the vote".On the afternoon of August 16, 2004, the day after the vote, Carter and Organization of American States (OAS) Secretary General César Gaviria held a joint press conference approving the preliminary results announced by the National Electoral Council. The monitors' conclusions ", coincided with the partial statements announced today by the National Electoral Council," Carter said, while Gaviria added that members of the OAS electoral observation mission had "found no element of fraud in the process." Directing his comments at opposition figures who made the allegations of "widespread fraud" in the vote, Carter called on all Venezuelans to "accept the results and work together for the future." However, an exit poll conducted by Penn, Schoen & Berland Associates (PSB) had predicted that Chavez would lose by 20%, when the election results showed a 20% victory, Schoen, commented, "I think it was massive fraud."

Following the breakdown of diplomatic relations between Ecuador and Colombia in March 2008, Carter brokered an agreement between the presidents of the two countries for the reestablishment of low-level diplomatic relations, which was announced on June 8, 2008.

Ideological positions

Criticism of U.S. policy

In 2001, Carter criticized the controversial pardon of Marc Rich, approved by President Bill Clinton, calling it "disgraceful" suggesting that Rich's financial contributions to the Democratic Party were a factor in Clinton's decision.

Carter has also criticized George W. Bush's presidency and the Iraq war. In a 2003 editorial in *The New York Times,* Carter warned against the consequences of a war in Iraq and called for restraint in the use of military force. In March 2004, Carter also accused George W. Bush and Tony Blair of waging an unnecessary war based on lies and misrepresentations to topple Saddam Hussein. In August 2006, Carter criticized Blair for being "subservient" to the Bush administration and accused Blair of giving unconditional support to Bush's Iraq policies. In May 2007 in an interview with the Arkansas Democrat-Gazette of Arkansas, he stated:

On May 19, 2007, Blair made his last visit to Iraq before resigning as British prime minister and Carter used the occasion to criticize him once again. Carter told the BBC that Blair was "apparently subservient" to Bush and criticized him for his "unconditional support" of the Iraq war. Carter described Blair's actions as "abominable" and said that "the British Prime Minister's almost unstinting support for President Bush's misguided policies in Iraq had been a great tragedy for the world. Carter said he believed that if Blair had distanced himself from the Bush administration in the run-up to the 2003 invasion of Iraq, he could have made a crucial difference to public and political opinion in America, and therefore the invasion would not have gone ahead. Carter expressed his hope that Blair's successor, Gordon Brown, would be "less enthusiastic" about Bush's Iraq policy.

In June 2005, Carter urged the closure of the Guantanamo Bay prison in Cuba, which has been a focal point for recent prisoner abuse claims.

In September 2006, Carter was interviewed on BBC Newsnight, a current affairs program, expressing concern about the growing influence of the Religious Right in U.S. politics.

On June 3, 2008, near the end of the primaries, Carter, as a former president, was named a superdelegate to the Democratic National Convention, announcing his endorsement of Senator and later President Barack Obama.

In 2009, he weighed in on Venezuelan President Hugo Chavez's accusations of U.S. involvement in the 2002 attempted coup d'état in Venezuela perpetrated by a civilian-military junta, stating that Washington knew of the coup and may have taken part.

Death penalty

Carter has continued to speak out against the death penalty in the United States and around the world. Most recently, in his letter to New Mexico Governor Bill Richardson, he urged him to sign a bill to eliminate the death penalty and institute life without parole. The bill passed the state House and Senate. Carter wrote:

Carter has also called for the commutation of the death penalty for many prisoners already sentenced, including Brian K. Baldwin (executed in 1999 in Alabama), Kenneth Foster (sentence commuted in Texas in 2007) and Troy Anthony Davis (from Georgia).

Abortion

Carter personally opposes abortion, although he supported its legalization after the historic 1973 U.S. Supreme Court ruling in Roe v. Wade, which recognized, albeit with limitations, the right to voluntary termination of pregnancy. One of the hot points during his electoral campaign for President was precisely the issue of abortion. As a candidate, under pressure from his advisors, he was unable to clearly state his position on the issue, and was therefore ambiguous, which earned him the criticism of both pro-abortion and pro-life currents.

Once installed in the White House, he adopted a pragmatic policy, choosing as his confidants women who were pro-choice, but appointing as Secretary of Health and Education Joseph Califano (who was against abortion) and increasing federal aid to family planning centers as an alternative to abortion. His lack of support for increased federal funding for abortions earned him criticism from the American Civil Liberties Union, which alleged that he did not do enough to find alternatives to this problem.

In subsequent statements, Carter stated:

Torture

In a 2008 interview with Amnesty International, Carter criticized the use of torture at Guantanamo Bay, saying it *contravenes the basic principles on which this nation was founded.* He said the next president should publicly apologize at his inauguration, and declare that the United States *would never again torture prisoners.*

Books

Carter has been a prolific author in his post-presidency, having written more than twenty books. Among them are the first fiction novel written by a former U.S. president,

The Hornets Nest, as well as one co-written with his wife, Rosalynn, and a children's book illustrated by his daughter, Amy. They cover a wide range of topics, including humanitarian work, aging, religion, human rights, and poetry.

Ministry

At the age of 18, he became a deacon at Maranatha Baptist Church in Plains, Georgia, where he taught Sunday school.

In 2007, he founded the New Baptist Alliance for Social Justice.

Personal and family life

During his presidency

His youngest daughter, Amy Carter, who was 9 years old when her father's presidency began, was the subject of constant media attention, for not since John F. Kennedy's presidency in the early 1960s had children lived in the White House.

After the presidency

In 2000, he announced that he had left the Southern Baptist Convention because of its rigid doctrines that no longer held true beliefs, while remaining a member of the Cooperative Baptist Association.

Carter and his wife, Rosalynn Carter, are also well known for their volunteer work with Habitat for Humanity, a Georgia-based philanthropy that helps low-income women workers build and buy their own homes. He is a Sunday school teacher and deacon at Maranatha Baptist Church in his hometown of Plains, Georgia.

Carter's hobbies include painting, fly fishing, woodworking, cycling, tennis and skiing.

The Carters have three sons, one daughter, eight grandchildren, three granddaughters, and two great-grandchildren. Their oldest son, Jack, was the Democratic candidate for U.S. Senate in Nevada in 2006, losing to incumbent John Ensign. Jack's son, Jason, was elected president of the Georgia State Senate in 2010.

Health problems

On August 12, 2015, he disclosed that he had been diagnosed with metastatic cancer after undergoing surgery to remove a tumor in his liver. He was treated with radiation therapy and pembrolizumab, a monoclonal antibody that boosts the immune system against tumors. Carter has an extensive family history of cancer, including his parents and siblings. A few months later, tests concluded that Carter was free of the disease.

On May 13, 2019, Carter broke his hip after suffering a fall at his Plains home and underwent surgery the same day at Phoebe Sumter Medical Center in Americus, Georgia. On Oct. 6, a forehead wound above the left eyebrow received during another fall at his home required 14 stitches.A public appearance later revealed that the former president had ecchymosis around his eye from the injury. On Oct. 21, Carter was admitted to Phoebe Sumter Medical Center after suffering a pelvic fracture when he again fell at home for the third time in the same year. However, he was able to resume teaching Sunday school at Maranatha Baptist Church on Nov. 3.

On Nov. 11, Carter was admitted to Emory University Hospital in Atlanta to relieve pressure on his brain caused by bleeding related to his falls. The surgery was successful and he was discharged on Nov. 27. On Dec. 2, Carter was hospitalized again for a urinary tract infection, but was released on Dec. 4.

On February 18, 2023, several years after his disease was under control, he relapsed again. He began to receive palliative treatments for his illness at home due to a growing picture of metastasis. Fearing an imminent death, the family released a statement for his loved ones, friends and the general public:

Longevity

Carter has been the longest living former president since the death of Gerald Ford in 2006. In September 2012, he surpassed Herbert Hoover as the oldest retired president. Carter became the longest-lived president to attend a U.S. presidential inauguration in 2017, at the age of 92, and the first to live to the 40th anniversary of his own inauguration. Two years later, on March 22, 2019, he became the oldest living former U.S. president when he surpassed George H. W. Bush, who died at the age of 94 years and 171 days in November 2018.

On October 1, 2019, Carter became the first former U.S. president to live to be 95. In 2019, in an interview for

People magazine, the former president noted how difficult it was to reach age 90 since he had never expected it, and that his secret to a long life was to have a good marriage. Carter had previously made arrangements to be buried at his Plains, Georgia home. In 2006 his funeral was planned to be in Washington D. C.

Other books by United Library

https://campsite.bio/unitedlibrary

Printed in the USA
CPSIA information can be obtained
at www.ICGtesting.com
LVHW012354031223
765486LV00016B/1287

9 789464 900729